THE
FUNNY SIDE
OF
BILLY CONNOLLY

THE
FUNNY SIDE

OF
BILLY CONNOLLY

BRUCE DESSAU

ORION
MEDIA

First published in 1996 by Orion Media

an imprint of Orion Books Ltd

Orion House 5 Upper St Martin's Lane, London WC2H 9EA

Copyright © Orion Books Ltd

Designed and created by The Bridgewater Book Company Ltd

A CIP catalogue record for this book is available from the British Library

ISBN 0752 80737 4

Printed and bound in Great Britain

by Butler & Tanner Ltd, Frome and London

CONTENTS

CHAPTER ONE

THE LITTLE BIG YIN IN GLASGOW • 6

CHAPTER TWO

BIG BANANA FEET AND OTHER STORIES • 20

CHAPTER THREE

LONDON CALLING • 38

CHAPTER FOUR

OH NO! THE BASTARD'S GOING TO SING • 58

CHAPTER FIVE

AMERICA: LEAD-FREE AND FART-FREE • 72

CHAPTER SIX

GOING BACK TO PISS ON OLD TREES • 84

THE LITTLE BIG
YIN IN GLASGOW

Billy Connolly is one of the finest and funniest comedians the
United Kingdom has ever produced. It's something you can't
argue about. Whatever you might think of Connolly's behaviour – and he has done and worn some strange things over the years –
no one in their right mind would question his comedic skills. He is a
wit, a raconteur, a master of the one-liner. He is also a bridge between
the old wave of comedy and the new wave, and a breaker of taboos. He
was talking about the very stuff of life back in the '70s when his rivals
were still talking about the weight problems of their mothers-in-law.

You could construct an argument in your sleep that Billy Connolly
was the godfather of alternative comedy, but this book isn't going to waste its time with
that. Instead it is simply going to tell the story of Connolly's life through his humour.
Because without getting too philosophical about things, it is clearly Connolly's humour
that has got him through life.

Yet it is a life that appears to have come full circle. Having spent the best part of a quarter of a century putting as many miles as possible between himself and his past, Connolly now seems to be coming home, both spiritually and physically.

Billy Connolly was born on 24 November 1942 on the kitchen-floor lino of 65 Dover Street in Anderston, Glasgow. According to Connolly's late mother, Mary, the birth was agony. Which was not surprising, given that the newborn William weighed in at 11 pounds and 4 ounces. He was a Big Yin, even as a baby...and he just kept on growing.

BELOW
Crowning glory: the King of Scottish comedy outside Buckingham Palace, June 1974.

It's comedy law that all great comedians have to suffer as children and Billy certainly had his fair share of problems. His family wasn't poor, but with the war on, money was tight. Anderston wasn't a slum, but it was no suburban paradise either. Connolly used to call it jokingly in later years 'a quaint fishing village on the banks of the Clyde'. When he had become successful and started staying in grand hotels, he would look back on his tenement childhood: 'I don't think I'll ever get used to big rooms. When I was a boy I could turn off the light and be in bed before it was dark.'

6 I don't think I'll ever get used to big rooms. When I was a boy I could turn off the light and be in bed before it was dark. 9

In 1946 Billy's mother walked out on her family, leaving his father William and two aunts to bring up Billy and his sister Florence. You don't need a PhD in psychology to work out that this had a profound effect on the young boy, particularly when it emerged years later that his aunts had been brutal surrogate parents. In a funny, yet painful, routine Connolly would show how kids get told off, miming being whacked on every syllable, and it wasn't hard to imagine that this, like many aspects of his act, was derived from his own experiences. It's an element of his act that younger comedians have identified with too – Sean Hughes used to do a similar routine in his shows.

What is hard, though, is to work out how many of Connolly's memories of his childhood are accurate and how many are the result of too much Californian therapy. But regardless of any psychobabble, Connolly's comic memories certainly ring true. The story of how Connolly first discovered the thrill of making other people laugh has an archetypal flavour to it. It was in the playground of St Peter's School and it had been raining. Connolly, who was about seven at the time, fell into a puddle and what might have been a humiliating experience suddenly turned into a joyous one when he realised he had made his friends laugh. In fact he found that he liked the sound so much (not to mention being the centre of attention) that he stayed in the puddle longer than was necessary. Then, as today, Connolly had an instinctive way of milking every last drop of humour out of a gag. And more importantly he had discovered something that made him forget his troubles at home. Thirty years later, in the *Sunday Express*, he would recall his formative experiences as the playground clown, as if they had happened yesterday: 'Their laughter was like oxygen to me and I never lost the need for it.' The fact that his first joke related to him getting his feet wet might also explain why wellies became something of a leitmotif in his professional act. In later years he would even sing a song in praise of wellies: 'If it wasnae for your wellies where would you be? You would have a dose of the flu or even pleurisy if you didnae have your feet in your wellies. They keep out the water and keep in the smell.'

Much of Connolly's schoolboy humour, however, was undistinguished. Like everybody else he knew, it seemed to revolve around bodily functions and the size of other boys' willies. Some of the gags lasted until adulthood, such as the mythical tale of the boy who could fart in stereo. Other gags just faded away, but Connolly was clearly inspired by the subject matter. As an adult he tried to explain the enduring

ABOVE
'Away and bite your arse.'
Connolly smiles and sees off
another critic.

~

9

ABOVE
**Connolly and the beard
that conquered Scotland.**

appeal of lavatorial humour in *Billy Connolly – The Authorized Version* (Pan, 1976). 'I know that some people find my talking about lavvies and jobbies and farting offensive, but there is a reason for it. Because when you are in a public lavvie, or a situation like that, you are vulnerable. And when you are vulnerable, you are funny.'

In his early teens, the Connolly clan moved out to Drumchapel, a greener but still urban area, known as 'the desert with windows'. Connolly's local football team was Partick Thistle FC, a team so unsuccessful that some people thought their name was Partick Thistle Nil. To the young Connolly, Glasgow was a grey, bland place architecturally – it didn't do much for the living but, looked after the dead. On the streets, with a mix of Irish and Scottish sensibilities, there was a rich seam of comedy everywhere you looked. Everyone was a wit. In later years Connolly told a story about the unhelpful bus conductor, who, when asked if the bus that said Drumchapel on the front was going to Drumchapel, replied that 'it said India on the tyres but it wasn't going there either.'

If school was a mixed experience, at least it gave Connolly some material for his act in later years. Although he had learnt to play the banjo there, he recalled on *On Tour With The Big Yin* (Castle Communications) that it hadn't all been fun.

'I hated school and the bit I hated the most was music. I think it's got more and more apparent in my playing. I hated my music teacher, she was bloody terrible. She was a psychopath. Totally addicted to "Marie's Wedding". Every music lesson we got "Marie's Wedding". You're sitting there with big holes in your jumper. Your wellies on. Singing "Step we gayly on we go". It was a right scruffy school. The uniform was wellies. She believed in all the modern teaching methods, like grabbing you by the back of the neck and smashing your nose on the desk.'

Connolly recalled how his class was divided into the Brylcreem crowd, who were always top, and the bottom bunch. Connolly was in the middle group – stupid but savable. Connolly's idea of a great poet wasn't Scottish bard Robert Burns, but William Miller, who wrote *Wee Willie Winkie*.

At St Peter's Secondary School he may not have been the class clown, but there was a clear sense that Connolly was setting himself apart from his peers. Though tall and fit, he was no aspiring hooligan, but neither was he a budding intellectual. Instead he was a bit of a daydreamer, prone to spending time alone and, hard as it is to believe now, he is remembered by contemporaries – if at all – as being on the quiet side.

As a teenager Connolly joined the scouts and developed a love of the countryside, which he still has today (and was possibly in the back of his mind when he adapted the Village People hit 'In the Navy' and re-recorded it as 'In the Brownies' in the late '70s). The young Connolly would get away from the city bustle by going camping and cycling around the more scenic areas on the outskirts of Glasgow.

Connolly loved the outdoor life. It didn't seem to bother him that the Scottish weather was so brutal. In later years he would say that there were only two seasons in Scotland – June and winter. As he grew up he would venture further afield. With his mates he would drive to the toll booth on the Forth Bridge and indulge in a local ritual, asking the man in the toll booth, 'How much?' When he said ten bob, Connolly would shout, 'Sold!'

In a city built on a mixture of fish suppers, Irn Bru, wit and machismo (as Connolly once said, 'Everybody in Glasgow is called Jimmy. Even the women'), he was a strangely reflective character. Maybe it was this contemplative side that made him consider becoming a Catholic priest.

❛ Another night a guest arrived at a party in Springburn, an area once famous for its steam locomotives, carrying so many fish suppers that the vinegar had pickled his willy. He proceeded to grab a large glass of brandy and dunk the member into the tumbler, with a yell of pain that could be heard in the next county. ❜

ON HOGMANAY

RIGHT
Comic strip: Connolly bares nearly all at the Hammersmith Odeon, New Year's Eve, 1979.

~

❛ If it wasnae for your wellies where would you be? You would have a dose of the flu or even pleurisy if you didnae have your feet in your wellies. They keep out the water and keep in the smell. ❜

ABOVE
Laughs with strings attached:
Connolly's folk background meant
that a guitar was never far away
during his early comic career.

For a while he also considered becoming a vet. But motivation was clearly a problem. When he left school at the age of sixteen, the only subject he had any qualifications in was engineering. Despite his comic talents and his undeniable instinctive ability to entertain, it looked las though Connolly was heading for the Clydeside shipyards that dominated Glasgow's skyline.

Connolly fought hard against his destiny at the docks. There were brief forays as a delivery boy, working for a bookshop and a bakery, but he started his welder's apprenticeship at Stephen's Yard in 1960. Even then he sneaked off twice to try to join the navy, attracted by the glamorous locations written on the side of the ships he saw being built, but his father spotted him and dragged him back to finish his apprenticeship. It would take Connolly five years to be fully qualified, but he was soon an accepted member of 'The Black Squad', the workers who would finish a long hard day caked in dirt.

If school taught Connolly the basics of humour, he graduated with a first-class degree in comedy banter while training as a welder. The yard was like a small village where everyone worked hard and played hard. Developing a tough sense of humour was the best way of coping and Connolly could never understand why the people he encountered at work were funnier than the people he saw on the television. Some of

OPPOSITE
A flare for comedy: it may have been
the mid-'70s, but for Connolly's
sleeves it was still 1972.

~

the characters who spent a lifetime on the Clyde could easily have had careers as entertainers but, like Connolly's, their language might not have been quite fitting for the BBC. There was the lad who would entertain his mates during breaks wearing a cape; another who had a cigarette on the end of a wire attached to his helmet so that he could smoke while his hands were full. The way Connolly remembers it, Stephen's Yard sounds more like the waiting room of *Broadway Danny Rose*.

There's an enduring myth that Connolly hated Scotland and couldn't wait to leave it, but this is clearly not true today, when he seems to return there at any opportunity to tour or to make a television programme. He has always loved fishing in Scotland. He once had an idea for catching salmon, which was to wear a crash helmet and nut them as they swam past, but it never caught on.

BELOW
**Connolly rarely drank before a show,
but afterwards was another matter.**

Even when he did seem a little estranged from his homeland and was living in England in the mid '80s, Connolly looked back fondly on certain Scottish traditions. Hogmanay, for instance, was always a special time. In *The Sunday Times* in 1984, Connolly recalled a special New Year when he was eighteen. 'I went first-footing on crutches because of a broken ankle sustained in a shipyard accident. I abandoned the crutches very early in the evening, showing the awesome curative powers of Bacardi and Coke, and trudged through the snow, from party to party, for the rest of the night, with my plaster growing ever softer and wider. Anyone coming across my footprints in

OPPOSITE
Definitely not a rendition of 'Marie's Wedding'.

BELOW
**Not just a stand-up comedian
but a lying-down one as well.**

the snow that night would surely have come to the conclusion that a one-legged drunk was being followed by a hopping yeti. I have no idea what became of the crutches. Perhaps some poor soul found them and came to the conclusion that he had witnessed some kind of miracle. For all we know, there may even be a grotto on the site.'

He also talked about an equally bizarre Hogmanay incident:

'Another night a guest arrived at a party in Springburn, an area once famous for its steam locomotives, carrying so many fish suppers that the vinegar had pickled his willy. He proceeded to grab a large glass of brandy and dunk the member into the tumbler, with a yell of pain that could be heard in the next county.'

Even washed and brushed up, and ready for a night down the dance halls (legend has it that Billy was a reserve for Scotland's *Come Dancing* team), the Billy Connolly of the early '60s looked very different from the Billy Connolly of the early '70s that everyone came to know. At this point Connolly had short hair, no beard and a penchant for pointed shoes that marked him out as something of a dandy among the *beau monde* of the Barrowland Locarno.

By 1965 Billy Connolly had qualified as a welder, but more importantly his ambitions were becoming more focused. During his time on the Clyde he had joined the Territorial Army. It was only part-time soldiering, but it did involve some parachuting, which earnt Connolly a red beret (he said it made him look like a spot) and also took him around Europe. He felt that it made him more macho, but he also thought it was a bit silly. Once his platoon went all the way to the Mediterranean on manoeuvres and after ten days the only soldier they had caught turned out to work in the same shipyard as Connolly; he felt he could have got him in the works canteen and saved the country all that money.

OPPOSITE
**If a routine required the
removal of clothing, Connolly
would oblige – as long as it
was artistically necessary.**

~

The travel wasn't completely wasted, though. It was in Nicosia one night that he decided to get up onstage. Given the fact that he had been honing his talents among his workmates for a number of years now, the big surprise was that he didn't actually do a stand-up act; instead he sang folk songs and plucked his banjo. It wasn't the career he had planned, but once again, the positive audience response confirmed that being onstage performing live was Connolly's natural habitat.

He was a changing man, and not just psychologically. By the mid-'60s the clean-cut, slick look had been replaced by a more familiar Connolly appearance, bearded and long-haired. For a while there was even a full beard, but a welding accident singed some skin on his right cheek and hair would no longer grow there. To match the sides up, Connolly shaved the other side and developed the distinctive Frank Zappa of Folk Music appearance.

After a 10-week stint building an oil rig in Biafra in 1965, Connolly felt ready to pursue a career in show business. As if tempting fate by living up to the stereotype of the canny Scot, he had salted away £700 and didn't need to find another welding job to pay the rent. Instead he strapped on his banjo and headed for the clubs, forming The Humblebums with Tam Harvey and setting off on the folk circuit. Connolly was on his way, even if he had misgivings about the scene and the genre, dubbing it 'three hairy pullovers singing about deid sailors'.

Connolly's inevitable move from folk music to comedy has become part of show business legend. After all those years of exchanging banter in the shipyards, Connolly wasn't going to be restricted to a few songs. He was soon confident that his comedy worked, when one night he fluffed an introduction to a song called 'St Brendan's Island' and found that he got a better response to the gags he told during the break than he did to the song when he finally completed it. As the line-up of The Humblebums changed, he was joined by

LEFT
The folk scene soon became a thing of the past, as Connolly grew in confidence as a solo performer.

ABOVE
**No more 'hairy pullovers',
but no haircut either.**

Gerry Rafferty, a man as shy as Connolly was confident. Rafferty wanted nothing more than to play his own compositions; Connolly wanted nothing more than to be the centre of attention telling gags.

Gradually what started out as amusing intros to folk songs became intros to original songs, then extended intros, then intros and outros, then intros and outros that were longer than the songs themselves. The band was doing very well, but Connolly had now found his voice elsewhere and was getting jaded with the folk scene. Despite some healthy album sales and even an appearance at a Royal Command Performance, Connolly didn't want to sing about 'deid sailors' for ever.

It seemed that music didn't satisfy him any more. Having complained about how everyone on the folk circuit did 'The Wild Rover', he looked into the cabaret scene and found that everyone there was doing the same numbers too – only this time it was 'Ten Guitars'. He clearly felt the need to do something more original to earn a living and make a name for himself. The music phase was doomed and in 1971 The Humblebums went their separate ways. Rafferty went on to greater musical success with Stealer's Wheel, while Connolly struck out as a solo performer, looking for gigs and bookings as a stand-up comedian. He had found his true vocation. Now all he had to do was be a success.

~

BIG BANANA FEET
AND OTHER STORIES

By 1971 Billy Connolly certainly looked like the Billy Connolly the world was going to fall in love with and laugh with. Onstage there was the Merlin hair in full flow, accompanied by some bright, florid, hippy threads. As Connolly became more confident he would add strange purple polka-dot pyjamas and a pair of yellow boots in the shape of bananas and create a lasting, if somewhat hallucinogenic, image. Still a dandy at heart, Connolly had actually wanted pink furry boots, but had opted for the banana skins that were to become his trademark – and provide the title for his 1976 live in-concert movie, 'Big Banana Feet'. It was an unusual look, which would have certainly seemed out of place in the shipyards. It would have looked out of place hanging around in Glasgow's folk bars. But Connolly the comic was able to carry it off onstage. The outrageousness of his verbals had found their perfect soulmate in the outrageousness of his clothes.

LEFT
Connolly puts the boot in.
Slip-ons, of course.

OPPOSITE
Still driving his fans bananas.

ABOVE
Connolly laughs at his own jokes, even though he has heard them before. They must be funny.

OPPOSITE
'So there was this wee police cadet from Maryhill...'

Connolly and his clothes have always had a strange relationship. To the outsider, Connolly's clothes – under his recent sober suits – often resembled an explosion in a Hawaiian shirt factory. Yet even in 1985, when he appeared on Channel 4 on *An Audience with Billy Connolly* (released on video by VVL), sporting a relatively subdued zebra-skin print, Connolly said that he was plain and had always done his best to look 'windswept and interesting'. He claimed that whenever he wore something expensive it looked stolen. Who was he trying to kid? With that beard and that hair Connolly would look striking in a duffel coat. It says something about the state of his self-esteem (and psychiatrists could probably qualify for an Arts Council grant for this one), which may have stemmed from his mother's departure when he was four, that Connolly, surely one of the most distinctive faces in modern comedy, could consider himself to be 'plain'.

Back in 1971, however, times were so tough that Connolly could only dream of wearing designer threads to attract attention. Never mind the banana boots, which Connolly could barely walk in (but which did get him a cheap laugh), Connolly couldn't even afford shoes and claimed later that he had had to convince himself that having holes in his sandals was trendy, just to cheer himself up. He was hardly a small star, let alone a huge star, and had a wife, Iris, and a son, Jamie, to support. He was prepared to take bookings as a comedian anywhere, for expenses only, and gradually he started to build up a following.

However determined Connolly was about stand-up comedy, he was already confident enough in his creative skills to work on a satirical show, to be performed initially in Glasgow and later at the 1972 Edinburgh Festival. The Great Northern Welly Boot Show was the kind of spoof saga that Spike Milligan might have concocted if he had grown up on the Clyde. The show satirised the shipbuilding industry – instead of teams of horny-handed workmen building ships, they were building that other famed Scottish industrial export, the wellington boot. Connolly co-wrote and performed the show (alongside future luminaries of Scottish drama such as Bill Paterson) and the production was such a success that it transferred to the Young Vic in London. The show helped to kick-start Connolly's career. In Scotland the ex-folkie found a new audience, while in England he found an audience for the very first time. Things were definitely looking up.

OPPOSITE
Family life: Billy, Iris, various kids, friends and pets.

BELOW
Braced for a good night. Connolly, as ever, settling in for a night onstage.

Over the next couple of years Connolly was constantly on the road, though he clearly found time to pop home every now and again – a daughter, Cara, was conceived between gigs. Jamie was now at school and rather proud of his father. While other dads were clerks, welders or businesss-men, Jamie could boast that his dad 'plays guitar and talks about jobbies'. A strange way for a grown man to earn a living, perhaps, but it was beginning to reap dividends.

There were still problems along the way. Connolly hadn't quite got his management sorted out in the early days, and in *Billy Connolly – The Authorized Version* he recalled how he had been taken advantage of. 'When I was finally beginning to make it, all sorts of lunatics wanted to manage me. And I actually took one on. One day I went into his office and he says to me: "What you need is a cheque book."...So I go down to the bank, blahbetty-blah, get my cheque book. So then he tells me it would be simplest if I left it with him in the office...and the next time I went into his office, he covered up this piece of paper he was writing on. Anyway, eventually I got a glance at it: he had written out my name about fifteen times, practising my sig-nature.' Eventually the manager was caught out when he took a colleague out for a meal and insisted on paying the bill with Billy's cheque book. Word got back to Billy, who realised very quickly that it was time to change managers.

By 1974 Connolly was a national trea-sure. So much so that when Scotland headed out for the World Cup in Germany, Connolly did the peace-time equivalent of entertaining the troops and entertained the team. They may

RIGHT
**The trappings of celebrity:
Billy gets on his bike.**

not have won the World Cup, as eternal optimists back home were predicting, they may not even have got very far, but at least they had a good laugh.

Connolly was gradually setting his sights on bigger goals. Towards the end of 1974 he was getting more and more attention from the English media, which wondered whether Connolly's accent and attitudes would travel. As the now-lapsed Catholic comic himself might have said, 'Does the Pope kiss tarmac?' The certifiably uptight *Guardian* had worries about his toilet humour. Would the anally repressed English get the gags? What the paper failed to acknowledge was Connolly's consummate timing. There is something about a brilliant comedian that means that, even if you don't grasp every word he is saying, the sheer rhythm, cadences and sound of his delivery are often enough to reduce grown men to hysteria. Plus there was the fact that Connolly had a habit of laughing at his own gags. Now, if he found the stories funny each night, having heard them all before, they must be funny.

ABOVE
Billy contemplates another jobbie joke.

Everyone apart from the press understood Connolly. He was now a rock-and-roll comic – a cross between a hippy headbanger and Max Miller. There was no language barrier. He had the ability to tell long, rambling shaggy-dog stories, but he could also bring the house down with a sharp one-liner. For a Gael-force Scot, Connolly has a love of language that has its roots in not just shipyard vernacular, but also in the books of the defiantly English P.G. Wodehouse, a favourite author of the comic.

It was an evocative act. At times it was hard to tell whether Connolly's anecdotes were entirely fictional or entirely factual. The truth was no doubt somewhere in between, but he had an unerring ability, for instance, to make everyone who heard his routine about 'Marie's Wedding' believe that his music teacher really was a psychopath.

Connolly was hot property. He was able to tap into a shared childhood past where every teacher had a nickname. He was also very good on adolescent romance – 'kissing for

LEFT

**A relaxing moment offstage
– still smiling, of course.**

❛ Land of polluted river

Bloodshot eyes and sodden liver

Land of my heart forever

Scotland the brave. ❜

CONNOLLY'S VERSION OF
'SCOTLAND THE BRAVE'

OPPOSITE

**Not quite so happy. But then would you
be grinning, if the cameraman asked you
to wear a bowler hat?**

THREE hours' he would shout – and just as good when it came to talking about the problems of a society where grown men had to be tough and were not allowed to show their emotions.

Connolly's most famous sketch was his 'Crucifixion' routine. It rarely offended his fans, because by the time they came to his show they knew of the routine, in much the same way that fans of a pop group will go along already familiar with their hit singles. Besides, Connolly invariably gave out a warning early on in the set: 'Don't be alarmed by the content of the act. It's me who is going to hell.' This didn't stop someone trying to hit Connolly on the nose during one show, bringing a whole new meaning to the term punchline. Connolly claimed he didn't mean to be blasphemous, but you couldn't help thinking the anarchist in him enjoyed upsetting the establishment.

In Connolly's version of the Crucifixion, it all takes place in the Saracen's Head Inn. All the Apostles are there, tearing lumps off the Mother's Pride. They all sit down at a big table, because they are all having trouble standing up by this time and the atmosphere is getting tense: 'See you, Judas, you're getting on my tits.'

ABOVE
**Live and Dangerous: Connolly with
another tour souvenir.**

The Crucifixion routine regularly slayed them in Scotland, and it had the same effect south of the border. In an extended sermon, Connolly explained that due to a misprint at the printers, people thought that biblical events had taken place in Galilee, when in fact they had taken place in Gallowgate in Glasgow. The routine was captured for posterity on *On Tour With The Big Yin!*: 'The door opens...crash! And in he comes. The Big Yin...with the long dress and the casual sandals..."Out all morning doing the miracles. I'm knackered. Gies a glass o'that wine. Nae kidding, son, I'm knackered...Take a look oot that door. There's nothing but deid punters walking up and doon with their beds under their arms..."'

Things continue as you might expect, but in a thick Scottish brogue:,'"One o'you is gooing tae shop me...and two big Roman polis is goin' to weech me right 'oot o here and into jail. And I'm going tae do a wonnight lie-in, and I'm going tae get up in the morning and say, first offence, I'm onto probation, nae bother. But a big Roman is goin tae come into my cell and say 'Probationum my arsium...'"'

The scene culminates with Jesus being crucified in his Y-fronts and a small Roman with a big spear coming up to him. With his hands restricted, 'The Big Yin' performs one more miracle – and pees on the Roman.

In the mid-'70s Connolly's pop-star status was confirmed in a literal sense. In 1974 his *Solo Concert* album was the biggest-selling album in Scotland since *Sgt Pepper's Lonely Hearts Club Band*. He also had a hit with 'D.I.V.O.R.C.E.' This was Connolly's irreverent reworking of the recent Tammy Wynette hit of the same name. While her version was a plaintive ballad about a mum having to spell out the vital words, because she didn't want her kids to know that she and her husband were breaking up, Connolly had to spell out words such as quarantine, shots and squirm so that the dog didn't understand them. When the song was played on the radio, some of the fruitier language wasn't just spelt out, it was bleeped out – and nothing helps to make a hit more than a spot of bleeping. The single promptly went to the top of the charts.

The world that Connolly created onstage was not that far removed from the world he had grown up in, in Anderston. A place where mums had crumpled tights, dads were out drinking cheap beer and kids' noses were always running. Drunks were everywhere, usually vomiting diced carrots, even though they couldn't remember eating any, and wearing urine-soaked trousers. Even if these hadn't been Connolly's own direct experience of family life, he had absorbed these images from the neighbourhood as if by a process of osmosis. Yet fans as far afield as Belfast and Bournemouth related to Connolly's humour. Who hadn't been sick and wondered in amazement at the colour and contents of their own vomit?

In January 1975 Connolly took the big step of playing the London Palladium. During the previous year, he had undertaken a tour of Scottish village halls and community centres. He even appeared at the notorious Barlinnie prison, which, he recalled afterwards, gave both Connolly and the inmates a boost: 'They've come through bad times and they are standing upright. Giving a guy like that a laugh is a big thing to be doing with yourself.' In retrospect it is easy to see these shows as a psychological limbering-up for the big breakthrough; ventures that may not have been good for the wallet, but were, in the comic's own words, 'good for the brain'.

The wallet was an issue when it came to playing the Palladium. It was a big personal risk, not just professionally but financially. There was no promoter – he and his manager put together £1,500 needed to hire the premier West End venue – not a fortune but not an amount to be sniffed at, either.

BELOW
Connolly in concert: songs, stories and some of the rudest material you'll ever have the pleasure to hear.

Cynics might have predicted that the audience would either be tiny or packed with homesick ex-pats. Although there was an element of the truth in the latter theory, there was a healthy smattering of southerners too.

Not everyone in the audience appreciated the humour. One heckler rubbed Connolly up the wrong way and got some special attention from the Big Yin, who shouted: 'You should get an agent pal. Why sit there in the dark handling yourself?' It was a classic put-down, which silenced any other aspiring hecklers and won over the sceptics. Not that it was an off-the-cuff remark. Connolly had an entire range of responses to the toughest of hecklers.

One thing that hasn't changed throughout Connolly's comedy career is that he has never rigidly scripted an act. Of course he has his set songs and his set routines, but you could see him on consecutive nights and hear the same material in a different order, not hear some gags and hear some entirely new ones too. Sometimes people would cheer for the Crucifixion routine, and if Connolly didn't feel like doing it he would shout, 'Give us three nails and I'll show you.'

Connolly doesn't just feed off the audience's responses, he feeds off his own momentum. For a man so keen on language, the pauses are as funny and as important as the words. It's during those pauses, when Connolly can often be seen laughing at his own punchlines, that he is also going off on a mental tangent, perhaps coming up with an entirely new segment of his act, which in future years will become a classic.

It is a skill that he honed back in the clubs and one that he has never lost. It is interesting to compare Connolly with a comedian such as Ben Elton. The latter's material may be more overtly alternative, but while both deal in the absurdities of human behaviour, their deliveries couldn't be more different. Elton, even as confident as he is now, doesn't dare pause for breath (a habit he picked up in his early days, when he was afraid to leave a gap in which a heckler might be able to interrupt him). Connolly, on the other hand, can seem positively nonchalant about his act, winning the audience over through his sheer effortlessness, where Elton wins them over through sheer force of personality. Both performers, of course, are not short of charisma. The difference is that, by the time Connolly started performing, he knew it.

If Connolly was loved by the Scots for his brutal honesty and his scabrous wit, his outspoken approach was also the thing that would upset them. For one part of his act he rewrote the anthemic 'Scotland the Brave'. Connolly's version had little chance of ever becoming a national anthem, but it did ring true:

'Land of polluted river
Bloodshot eyes and sodden liver
Land of my heart forever
Scotland the brave.'

RIGHT
Billy looks heavenwards for inspiration? Not when he's doing the Crucifixion routine, though.

❛ You should get an agent, pal. Why sit there in the dark handling yourself? ❜

TO A HECKLER

With the Palladium under his belt, there was no stopping Connolly. He was also keen to have a stab at acting, filming *Just Another Saturday*, a BBC drama written by an old Clydeside colleague Peter McDougall, which set out to debunk the mythology of the Glasgow hard man.

In 1975 the time seemed absolutely right for Billy Connolly to make it big. What he was doing seemed on the one hand in tune with current trends in comedy, while on the other hand he represented a kick up the backside of the complacent comedy mainstream. Television comedy in the mid-'70s was dominated by the dickie-bow brigade, people like Bernard Manning and Jimmy Tarbuck. Their stock-in-trade was the mother-in-law and wife gag. Connolly disliked Bernard Manning in particular, not just because of his material but because Manning had been critical of Connolly. In his early days, many people compared Connolly to Lenny Bruce, because of his brutal honesty. This started to get Connolly down until he decided that it could be worse, they could be comparing him to Bernard Manning.

On the one hand, then, there were the mainstream reactionary comics, for whom Connolly had little time. But at the same time, unbeknown to Connolly, there was also a wave of provincial comics emerging in other cities, who came out of their respective folk scenes and had a similar, if gentler, approach to the Big Yin. The importance of folk music to '70s comedy cannot be under-estimated – the connection is simple; folk music is all about telling stories and the new strain of comedy that developed was also more about stories than one-liners. It was no surprise then, that apart from Connolly in Scotland, there was also Max Boyce in Wales, Mike Harding in Rochdale and Jasper Carrott in Birmingham. All moved from music into mirth-making, coming on, like you-know-who, with their guitars and mixing songs with hilarious tales. And all, like Connolly, were to go from being local heroes to national celebrities within a short space of time. Carrott and Harding even followed Connolly into the pop charts with their spoof hits 'Funky

LEFT
**The clown jewels: a
national treasure.**

Moped' and 'Rochdale Cowboy' respectively. It was as if Connolly had kick-started a new wave all his own – in reality it was clearly that the time was right for comedy to be shaken up and Connolly, above all, was in the right place at the right time. Something that was never more true than when he turned up at the BBC Television Centre in White City to make his début appearance on Michael Parkinson's chat-show in 1975. For anyone who already knew Connolly, his appearance on Parkinson's legendary show was anything but an overnight success. But for anyone who didn't know the comic, this was a historic television moment. And it all happened by chance.

In 1975 icon Michael Parkinson was travelling to Edinburgh Airport in a taxi when the driver insisted that he stop off and buy a copy of Connolly's album. Parkinson duly obliged, if only so that he wouldn't be taken on a scenic detour and miss his flight. Back in England, he only got round to listening to the album when his son mentioned it to him. Parkinson was struck by the immediacy of the humour and booked Connolly onto his top-rating show.

These days chat-show hosts are always introducing guests and predicting big things for them, only to see the acts promptly sink without a trace. Parkinson predicted big things for Connolly and for once the predictions came true.

The Big Yin certainly made an impression on the Saturday night BBC1 audience, who, weaned on a diet of variety specials and bland American imports, must have wondered what they were hearing when this hairy Scotsman sat down and started to tell Parkinson about this man who had murdered his wife. It was a risky gag. Connolly looked slightly nervous when he started telling it, but he carried on regardless and proceeded to inform the BBC viewers that the man buried his wife in the yard, with her bottom sticking out of the ground. After all, he needed somewhere to park his bike! These days a gag like that would prompt a hail of complaints – at the time it won Connolly a whole new nation of friends.

If the murdered wife's bum-gag suggested that Connolly was sexist, one should bear in mind that women also got the upper hand in Connolly's humour, long before political correctness came along. In some gags Connolly even ingeniously managed to combine casual brutality and post-feminist revenge, as in the story about the Glasgow sherrif who asks a woman why she shot her husband with a bow and arrow. Apparently she did it because she didn't want to wake the kids.

The Parkinson appearance was such a success that Connolly returned later that year in the run-up to his London shows at the New Victoria Theatre (he made ten appearances in all, a record). The TV turn helped to boost the profile of his shows, and one newspaper made a bold, double-edged prediction for Connolly: 'He'll probably end up with a season in Las Vegas, a TV series and a lost sense of humour.'

The tabloid soothsayers weren't right, of course, but Connolly has proved them wrong in ways that not even Mystic Meg would have dared predict. He didn't have a season in Las Vegas, but he would make a few Hollywood movies; he did have a TV series, but not the stand-up one that the

~

papers might have predicted – instead he would present art and travel shows. As for the lost sense of humour, if Billy Connolly was going to lose his sense of humour, he would have to be a very absent-minded comic indeed, and Connolly was far too sharp for that.

❛ The Big Yin certainly made an impression on the Saturday night BBC1 audience, who, weaned on a diet of variety specials and bland American imports, must have wondered what they were hearing when this hairy Scotsman sat down and started to tell Parkinson about this man who had murdered his wife. It was a risky gag. Connolly looked slightly nervous when he started telling it, but he carried on regardless and proceeded to inform the BBC viewers that the man buried his wife in the yard, with her bottom sticking out of the ground. After all, he needed somewhere to park his bike! These days a gag like that would prompt a hail of complaints – at the time it won Connolly a whole new nation of friends. ❜

RIGHT
Success by the book. Connolly's career trajectory continues – where to now?

CHAPTER THREE

LONDON CALLING

During his London shows in 1975 Connolly talked about his meteoric rise to the Sunday Express. *Despite having finally achieved what he set out to capture, stardom still seemed to have sneaked up on him and he didn't quite know what to make of it. Maybe, behind the bull-headed confidence, there still lurked the obligatory comedian's insecurity:* 'I was too scruffy for the theatre and too folksy for the cabaret. The truth of the matter is that I didn't fit in. People just didn't know what to make of me or my sense of humour. And can you blame them? I mean, look at me. Do I look like somebody who is currently the toast of London?'

RIGHT
Smartening up his image.

OPPOSITE
Connolly in his working gear again, stripped down to braces and basics for another live show.

~

RIGHT
Life was good for Billy, Iris and their two children, Jamie and Cara, even though the comic spent a long time on the road.

It was all a long way from his hard times trying to establish himself in London, which had now taken on a romantic, rose-tinted hue: 'Three years ago I was living in Finchley and was so broke I didn't know how I was going to pay for my next meal.'

By 1976 Connolly knew he was a success. He also knew that success could be a problem for someone who had based his material around growing up in a working-class environment. At the beginning of the year he, Iris, Jamie and Cara had moved from Glasgow to a much larger house only a short walk from Loch Lomond. If Billy Connolly hadn't become Squire Connolly just yet, he was certainly aware that his fans would feel that he was progressively moving in that direction.

This wasn't just a class issue; it also had a bearing on his act. There was always that fear that, as someone separate from the crowd, he would not have the universal experiences that were the essential raw ingredients of his act. It's the Catch-22 that rock groups had always experienced – your first album is all about life on the street, but by the time you try to write the follow-up you only ever see the street through the smoked-glass windows of a limousine – but Connolly was the first rock-and-roll comic and had to negotiate his way through uncharted waters. He may not have been a street comic, but he was certainly a bar-room comic and he could no longer simply hang out anonymously in pubs, picking up nuggets of conversation that he could then craft into beautiful stage stories. This was the kind of eavesdropping that writer Alan Bennett would also do, but where Bennett was bookish and retiring, the kind of person who could pass unnoticed among the public, Connolly's attention-grabbing appearance and his accompanying fame meant that he could no

OPPOSITE
Back on the road again, with a (non-alcoholic) drink for company. The Big Yin and a little drink.

LEFT
'Fame has it's drawbacks, but when
it comes to being noticed by people
on the street, it's quite lovely...'
Connolly on celebrity.

❝ When they put teeth in
your mouth, they spoilt a
perfectly good bum. ❞

TO A HECKLER

longer be just another customer. It was more likely that he would have to fend off fans offering him
terrible jokes than just overhear things. Though it would be unfair to say that fans burdened
Connolly with stinkers. Twenty years after he had told it to Parkinson, he claimed that the gag
about burying his wife with her bottom sticking out of the ground had been given to him. Then
again, bums had always been a great source of humour for Connolly. He had mentioned the word
in his version of 'D.I.V.O.R.C.E'. and one of his favourite heckler put-downs was 'When they put
teeth in your mouth they spoilt a perfectly good bum.'

Of course, greater success could also provide new sources for his act. Connolly's flying routine
was the kind of material he would never have come up with, had he stayed in Partick all his life.
One of Connolly's greatest aeroplane stories has since become a genuine urban myth. In a section
called 'The Jobbie Weecha', Connolly told the story of a Spaniard who turned up bruised and bat-
tered on 'the spam belt' of Edinburgh. It turned out that he had been a passenger in an aeroplane
flying over Scotland, and the machine that is supposed to throw the excrement out of the plane
threw the passenger out of the plane instead. The amazing thing was that it was a routine inspired
by flying, but the way Connolly told it, it was funny even if the listener had never left the ground.

This was another reason for Connolly to be worried about flying. He never did like it and talked
about having to have a few pints of foaming ale and some nippy sweeties (whiskies) for Dutch
courage before take-off.

ABOVE
'...It's a proof you exist. That all
the practising with the banjo in
your bedroom paid off.'

Travel had broadened his mind and sense of humour, and had helped him to come up with a whole new set of universal worries. Why, for instance, was there a lifejacket and not a parachute under the seat? Why did the stewardesses tell you to hold a cushion if the plane was about to collide with a mountain – were the passengers supposed to throw the cushions at the mountain simultaneously and shout, 'Go away, nasty mountain'?

But most of all, Connolly's flying routines revolved around the activities in the toilet. Why, for example, was there no window in the toilet – who on earth was going to see in? And then of course there was his biggest fear. Not crashing, but the fear that you might go into the toilet and there would already be a jobbie in the bowl that wouldn't flush away. You could hardly leave and say to the next person in the queue that it wasn't yours.

The problem of success as told to the *Daily Mail*: 'If money changes me, I'll just go ahead and change and be funny that way. I've no ambition to be out there where I come from. I've lived there and I don't like it. I get fed up with people talking about the shipyards. I've been in show business longer than I was a welder. I don't want to be known as the comedian who used to be a welder.'

By the time Connolly returned to the London Palladium in January 1976 there was a different crowd waiting to cheer him on. Of course there was the ex-pat contingent, but it had to fight for tickets with Connolly's new-found English fan club. As he arrived onstage he made a statement of intent, which made his position in the pantheon of tartan gag-makers perfectly clear: 'I come to bury Harry Lauder, not to praise him.'

Connolly then stepped out from behind a cardboard cut-out and proceeded to bring the house down. But it was this iconoclastic gesture that hit the right note and made things so much easier. Unwittingly Connolly may have looked like a hippy stopping off on his way to Stonehenge, but he was in perfect harmony with the anarchic punk spirit beginning to circulate around London that year. Lauder was a comedy dinosaur (admittedly dead, so an easy target), who had made his living out of a tried-and-tested array of kilt-and-sporran gags. The thought of Connolly in a kilt would have sent even his most ardent fans running for the hills. Though fans with a good memory might have noted that Connolly did wear a sporran – albeit in jest – when he first appeared on Michael Parkinson's show. He did quickly remove it, though.

At the Palladium Connolly also showed that he was aware of an ideological sea-change in comedy. He didn't mind the kind of crudity that would make Max Miller seem like a choirboy, but racism in comedy was a different kettle of fish. While the likes of Bernard Manning and the up-and-coming Jim Davidson were thriving on a diet of undistilled race gags, Connolly tried to distance himself from that sense of humour, in a way that only Connolly could: 'I'm not going to tell any more Irish jokes, they've taken enough stick. So, there were these two Laplanders, and one of them said to the other, he said, "Moichael".'

OPPOSITE
'Daddy, why does the doctor want my pee? Does he taste everybody's urine?'

~

LEFT
'I'd like to do more films. I'd
even shave my beard off if I had
to.' Connolly considers his
beard's prospects.

OPPOSITE
Beardless he got to the movies – well,
the cinema where *Braveheart* was on
for starters.

❛ I'm not going to tell any more

Irish jokes, they've taken enough

stick. So, there were these two

Laplanders, and one of them said

to the other, he said, 'Moichael'. ❜

If Connolly's attitude was punkish, his musical friends certainly weren't. Due to management connections, he toured America with Elton John that summer. He was the ultimate rock-and-roll comedian, playing to a crowd of 80,000 at New York's Madison Square Gardens. It wasn't a complete success, though. On the first night in Washington, Connolly was hit in the forehead by a smoking pipe. Reflecting on it in a television interview later, he said that the Americans made him feel as welcome as a fart in a spacesuit. America did give him a taste for the big-time though, but he had to reconcile that with the fact that he missed his family and Scottish curry.

In the spring of 1976 he renewed his professional relationship with Peter McDougall. Following the success of *Just Another Saturday*, they began filming *The Elephant's Graveyard*, a mordant, bleak drama about unemployment in Glasgow. It was the kind of story that Billy, for all his frippery and pop-star hobnobbing, could relate to. By the late '70s the shipyards around the Clyde were rapidly shrinking and the dole queues were growing. Connolly, though, had stayed more than a few steps ahead of the recession. He had never gone into comedy to avoid unemployment, but his uncanny knack of reinventing himself – a skill that he would utilise continually over the next twenty years – had kept him at the top of the pile. His engineering apprenticeship wasn't much use to him now,

ABOVE
'To an artiste, applause is like a banquet. Thanks for the cheese sandwich.'

OPPOSITE
A very rare picture of Billy Connolly: the comedian in a sober suit and tie.

but he joked that he had acquired some other essential skills at the University of Life: 'I'm a fully qualified survivor.'

Survivor or not, Connolly was still pretty self-effacing about his chances of becoming accepted as part of the golf-playing, charity-gigging, comedy establishment. That September he told the *Yorkshire Post*: 'I like show-business people. But I don't think you will ever see a Billy Connolly Spectacular and I doubt whether you will ever see me on *This Is Your Life*. I'll never get a knighthood.' Interestingly, he didn't actually say that he didn't want those things, he just suggested that he didn't expect them.

In 1980 Connolly appeared on *This Is Your Life*. It was a particularly strange affair, which became even stranger when host Eamonn Andrews introduced an anecdote from one of Connolly's old friends from the shipyards.

A doddery old man appeared on the screen, trotted out a story about Connolly's wisecracking welding days and then appeared in the studio. As if on cue, Connolly stood up and hugged the old man, as if they were a long-lost father-and-son double act. As it happened, the researchers seemed to have come up with the only man on Clydeside whom Billy had never actually met, but the star went along with the routine so as not to spoil the show.

As 1976 rolled on, Connolly was discovering that his humour did have the ability to travel, to places he never expected it to. Although Australia was an English-speaking country, it was still a relief to the performer that his tour went down a storm there. As he had found, first in England and then in America with Elton John (at least when the rock audience had paid attention to him), he was rapidly discovering that his local observations were a legitimate comedy currency anywhere in the world. Anyone who could understand English could understand his rich vein of raw domestic

~

humour. Connolly was doing what any great comic would
do and embellishing something that had a grain of truth in
it, such as when he did a mock interview with himself about
his Glasgow past: 'People say you were brought up in
Glasgow, Mr Connolly. In tenement life wasn't there a sense of community?' 'Sure, when there's
sixty-five of you sharing the toilet, it never has a cold seat.' The important thing is that if it didn't
have that grain of truth, it wouldn't have produced a rich harvest of laughs.

His toilet humour, of course, worked everywhere. And it was a subject dear to Connolly's heart.
Or trousers, to be more accurate. He may not have shown it very often, but Connolly was prone
to nervousness before a show. He didn't like to drink before he went on and, once onstage, performance was like a release.

According to Connolly, there was nothing like an important gig to loosen the bowels. As he said
after a particularly nerve-racking show: 'It's been super playing for you, but I must say it's the best
laxative I've ever had in my life.'

ABOVE

'I washed my hair last night – I cannae do a thing with the sink.'

As Billy Connolly became more successful he inevitably attracted the attention of politicians, who wanted to be associated with him, in the hope that some of his popularity would rub off on them during election time. The Scottish National Party had constantly tried to woo the comic – to no avail – and only the Labour Party had any success. Connolly appeared at some by-elections, which brought a smile to the faces of the Labour candidates, even if they did not win their seats.

As for the Scottish National Party, in 1977 Connolly was as scathing about them as ever, suggesting that the initials stood for 'Still Nae Policies'. It seemed rather unfair, but it did underline his ambivalent attitude to Scotland. He loved the country, but he did not necessarily want to spend the rest of his life there.

~

Connolly's growing fondness for England was also manifesting itself. The Scottish *Sunday Mail* had been running a Big Yin cartoon strip, which had proved a winner and boosted its circulation. But now Connolly decided he wanted to kill off his character. This could have been because he wanted to be taken more seriously, but a more likely reason was that in the cartoon Connolly was portrayed as a nationalist English-hater. Connolly's attitude was that it was perfectly acceptable behaviour to hate the English when they were playing the Scots at rugby at Murrayfield, but it was hard to hate them on a full-time basis.

Connolly had no time for racist humour, but neither did he have time for anything too high-brow. Not for the Big Yin the then-modish bizarre surrealism of Monty Python: 'My comedy doesn't leave you with brain damage or turn you into a pervert. It's like guys talking to each other. At least its real.'

His comedy skills were improving all the time. Still refusing to script his routine – the most he would do is have, say, twelve topics loosely planned – he felt he was a bit like a jazz musician

BELOW
'Stardom is something made up by journalists. I'm not even famous.' Connolly in modest mode.

(I've never worn a kilt seriously in my life. I'm a great patriot, but I think something like sporran rot set in.)

TO THE *NEWS OF THE WORLD*

improvising a solo off the top of his head. On his UK tour of 1977 he put this philosophy to the test and proved that he hadn't lost his touch, adding little local embellishments throughout the tour. In Leeds, for instance, he laid into the religious programme *Stars on Sunday*, which was filmed there, while in Wales it was Welsh choirs that were on the receiving end of Connolly's barbed wit. For someone who could be consistently funny, he admitted in an interview that it was a skill he might not always possess: 'My philosophy is do it when it hits you, because tomorrow it might not be there.' It was a strangely revealing hint of comic insecurity, particularly as it had come from one of the hottest comics in the country.

That summer Connolly undertook a seaside tour before appearing in London again. It was said that he chose the venues by sticking pins into the coastline. It may have sounded like a tacky end-of-the-pier show, but by now the star could do things in style, travelling in a limousine, where once a bus or coach would have been the height of luxury. The timetable took in such delights as Whitley Bay, Clacton, Skegness and Paignton, on the way to the Glasgow Apollo and London's Rainbow Theatre. Once again he hinted that his sympathies were moving south of Hadrian's Wall when he remarked that 'Any nation that invents train-spotting and the Royal Pavilion at Brighton has got to be a bit special.' Ideally he wanted frontiers knocked down, not put up, and he believed that that was what he was doing with his comedy, but that didn't stop him from feeling anxious about his coastal jaunt.

Connolly was particularly worried at the prospect of Torquay: 'I died on my arse the last time I played Torquay. It was a convention of Rotarians in a huge tent, and they gave me a bingo caller's microphone,' he told Michael Parkinson in *The Sunday Times*. Naturally he went down a storm. It was all a long way from Madison Square Gardens with Elton John, where he recalled that nerves had nearly got the better of him: 'The first time I went on there were more people sitting behind me than I'd ever had in front of me in all my life. Every night before I went on I'd vomit into a fire bucket.' As he might have said himself, 'It's no the eighteen Guinnesses, it's the diced carrots.'

The 1977 Extravaganza Tour was said to be the largest-ever tour of Great Britain by a stand-up comedian. Connolly may have been travelling in a limousine for parts of the journey, but that didn't stop him from shamelessly romanticising his occupation as a late twentieth-century wandering minstrel: 'I suppose we are all tarmac junkies hooked on the M1 and exhaust fumes, and waiting to mainline on Forte's motorway meat pasties again.'

Onstage he was as confident, assured and scriptless as ever. There were always a few topics for emergencies, if things looked bad, but by and large Connolly would go where his wit took him, chatting about first dates, waxing lyrical about the problems of shaving around pimples and wanting to put your arm around your girlfriend in the cinema.

There was one subject, one bodily function, that the comic always returned to. The real problem when you were courting in the cinema was not getting your arm round the back of the seat,

~

~

but what did you do if, once you got it there, you wanted to fart? The only option was to clench those buttocks and escape to the foyer. It was a routine that didn't just tell superbly; he did the mime and the sound-effects too.

As the '70s drew to a close it appeared that Connolly could do, if not no wrong, very little that would upset his ascent. North of the border he seemed as popular as Robbie Burns and his hero William Wallace rolled into one, while south of the border he could evoke hysteria simply by adapting a familiar song and putting daft words into it. One of his favourites was the country number 'I've been so lonesome in my saddle since my horse died' while Ian Dury's 'Hit me with your rhythm stick' turned into 'Hit me with your greasy chip' and little Jimmy Osmond's 'Long-haired lover from Liverpool' turned into 'Short-haired police cadet from Maryhill'. It was puerile. It was playground humour *par excellence*. Everyone from the age of six to ninety-six seemed to love it.

The ex-welder was now making a mint out of willies, wellies, wee-wees and jobbies. And, of course, that old faithful, the Glasgow drunk, a character who would stare out a chip if he thought it was giving him a funny look: 'Have you ever noticed about the Glasgow drunk, he walks with one leg like that [juts out leg]...fish supper in one hand, bottle of beer in his left-hand pocket...He keeps walking in circles...annoying everyone in the bus queue with "Yew all right...eh? Eh...how are yew...?"'

But behind the scatalogical humour there was a great deal of thought. The humour about religion might have been called blasphemous by his critics, but Connolly was actually trying to show the workings of religion – if 2,000 years of Christianity couldn't survive a gag about Jesus being Scottish, it was in a pretty poor state indeed. Connolly's early experiences of religion, when he discovered that the Catholic and Protestant schools studied from different history books, was still a sharp memory. Similarly he took the mickey out of royalty; just because he would later become friendly with the Windsors didn't mean that he thought the notion of monarchy and people's reactions to it weren't rather strange. Ultimately it was hypocrisy that Connolly hated; he recalled that the Duke of Edinburgh visited the shipyard once, and just before he came the workers had to clear everything up, paint white lines and put down instant grass. Connolly hated the pretence.

By 1977 Connolly was clearly keen to stretch himself. That year Peter McDougall's *The Elephant's Graveyard* was broadcast by the BBC. In it, Connolly played an unemployed Glaswegian, hanging around the park because he couldn't bear to tell his wife he hadn't got a job. It was a grim, demanding part, even though Connolly could identify with the character quite easily. Perhaps in some parallel universe there is a Billy Connolly who never left the shipyards when he finished his apprenticeship, but was forced to leave when the shipyards – along with most of Scotland's heavy industry – closed down. Maybe it was this sense of identification with his character which inspired such a great dramatic performance from Connolly.

OPPOSITE
If Robbie Burns had come from Maryhill and had worked on the shipyards and been looked after by his aunties, he might have been as funny as Connolly. But probably not.

~

Alongside a burgeoning television career, Connolly also accepted a role in the film *Absolution*, starring Richard Burton. Connolly played a wild-haired hippy – nothing too demanding. He recalled later how he and the film icon hit it off: 'When we met I was wearing jeans and wellies and I looked like an unemployed window-cleaner. He was dead smart in a mink jacket, but by the end of filming we were great mates.'

Unfortunately *Absolution* wasn't British cinema's finest hour. *The Monthly Film Bulletin* called it 'a dire slice of clever-clever narrative trickery'. But at least Connolly got to work alongside the husband of Elizabeth Taylor, teaching Burton how to sit in a confessional box, and in the process discovering that his Catholic upbringing wasn't entirely wasted.

By the end of 1978 Connolly was coming up with even more surprises, appearing with the Scottish Opera in *Die Fledermaus*. Fears that Connolly might sing were unfounded, as he was cast as Froisch, a jolly joking jailer.

It is one of the perks of celebrity that you get offers to appear in all sorts of projects, whether you seem qualified for them or not. It clearly makes sound commercial sense for the producers, too. Connolly's opera début no doubt put some opera virgins' bums on seats, and in December 1980 he even made his début on children's television. Jon Pertwee had created the cult of *Worzel Gummidge* and makers Southern Television, deciding that Worzel needed a northern companion, called on Connolly to play Bogle McNeep, the tartan terror. Harsh critics might have said that the sartorially questionable comic didn't need a special outfit for the part, but just to be on the safe side he was given carrot-coloured hair, a thistle for a nose and kipper boxes for boots. And perhaps most controversially, they managed to coax Connolly into a kilt. Rather like an actress doing nude scenes 'because they are in dramatic context', he could at least argue that he was wearing Scottish national dress because it was in keeping with his character.

While Connolly's tours were a sell-out, television still beckoned, but there was no way he could do his live act unexpurgated on the box. Did his Worzel Gummidge appearance suggest a new direction for the new decade? Now approaching forty, was Connolly about to become an all-round family entertainer?

OPPOSITE
**A contented Connolly. A national
star, a versatile performer and still a
hilarious comedian.**

CHAPTER FOUR

OH NO! THE BASTARD'S GOING TO SING

One of the intriguing gaps in Connolly's career has been the enduring problem of finding a suitable place for the comic on television. On Worzel Gummidge *he had a script, but there was little scope in the schedules for his own extended routines. Even though he was speaking universal truths that anyone could identify with, television companies have consistently found it hard to harness that raw power for a mainstream audience. Over the years various ideas had been suggested – a sitcom set on an oil rig and written by Peter McDougall had proved unworkable, a look at the world of advertising had been turned down. It was as if television only really wanted what it couldn't have – Connolly's no-holds-barred live act.*

ABOVE
Who says I'm Britain's worst dressed man? Connolly shocks a nation of tailors by sporting a suit.

OPPOSITE
Still able to chuckle, despite the slings and arrows of the Scottish tabloids.

Too young to be a father figure to the comedy new wave, Connolly was respected like an elder brother. Joined here at Amnesty International's twenty-fifth birthday party by Alexei Sayle, Pamela Stephenson and Lenny Henry.

The Parkinson breakthrough had proved how important television was for Connolly's career. Unsurprisingly, even before Parkinson, television had given him an early break when he had been booked to do a musical turn on a local programme, *Dateline Scotland*. In grand showbiz style a guest didn't turn up and the production team were at a loss. Until, that is, newsreader Reginald Bosanquet, who was on that night, mentioned that he had been chatting with Connolly backstage and the folk singer seemed to have a head packed with comic anecdotes. The producer allowed Connolly to talk, and he talked and he talked and he talked. For the first time the local minor celebrity known for his music looked capable of become an international major celebrity known for his gift of the gab. Nearly a decade on, Connolly was now looking for another way of breaking onto the box.

The early '80s marked a sea change in comedy. The late '70s punk credo that anyone could do it had moved from music to performance, and drama students, anarchists and performance artists began setting up their own comedy clubs. If there was a risk that this might sweep away the older comics, Connolly needn't have worried. He had been alternative before the word was invented. To some it even seemed as if he had invented the term. As someone who didn't fit the light entertainment template, Connolly, for all his wealth, was defiantly anti-establishment.

~

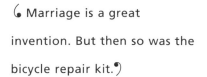

❝ Marriage is a great invention. But then so was the bicycle repair kit.❞

CONNOLLY LINE NOW IN THE OXFORD DICTIONARY OF QUOTATIONS

RIGHT
Billy and Pamela: the tabloids may have been critical, but the Scot and the woman from Down Under were the perfect showbiz couple.

The new wave didn't depose Connolly, because he didn't belong to the old wave and was conscious of this in their presence. In 1980 he appeared at the *Secret Policeman's Ball*, an Amnesty International fundraising show in London. Alongside assorted Pythons, Footlights' veterans and alternative alumni, Connolly was undeniably sensitive about being different. Even if they weren't ex-public school, the new wave of comedians had degrees: Connolly took the question of upbringing by the scruff of the neck, making a virtue out of the fact that, as he said, 'I think I'm the only person here who wasn't at school until he was twenty-one.'

The year of 1981 was a tough one for Connolly. He split from his wife Iris and his relationship with Pamela Stephenson became public knowledge, making their relationship tabloid fodder. Connolly's marriage to Iris had lasted a lot longer than many showbiz marriages, but his protracted absences on tour had taken their toll. While she lived in their house in Loch Lomond and entertained their kids, he had often been on the other side of the world, entertaining his fans It was a difficult situation, even before Pamela Stephenson appeared.

While the break-up and the blonde, attractive Stephenson made Connolly's often fraught relationship with the press more fractious than ever, he tried to deflect attention from his private life by throwing himself into his work. There was a UK tour, a world tour, charity work and an appearance in a dress alongside Kenny Everett.

~

The madcap DJ had invited Connolly to join him in a sketch in which they played a couple of dotty dowagers having tea. Connolly was no doubt anxious. Last time he had appeared on a show with Everett the previous year, it had been a set-up to get him into a TV studio and spring *This Is Your Life* on him. With Everett, anything could happen. In fact the main problem was that the duo found the idea of cross-dressing so hilarious that Connolly kept cracking up and the scene had to be filmed repeatedly. When the punchline finally came – Kenny wanted to point out that Billy had a facial hair problem – it must have been a great relief to all involved.

He was particularly concerned about itchy bottoms, and wondered why they always occurred in public and at the least convenient times. As Connolly observed with great relish, you never get an itchy bum in the middle of a desert. The comic suggested a few options, which included trying

BELOW
Back on the chain gang: Connolly indulges in some convict-related capers.

funny walks and clenching your buttocks, before suggesting the ultimate solution: to own up very loudly to having an itchy bum, so that everyone looks away in embarrassment and you can deal with it in private.

By the summer of 1982 Connolly was something of a veteran of the London stage, but one thing he had yet to do was appear in a West End play. His chance came that July when he was offered the opportunity to take over from Simon Callow in the lead role in J.P. Donleavy's *The Beastly Beatitudes of Balthazar B,* at the Duke of York's Theatre. It is unclear whether Connolly had ever seen Callow's performance as the drinking, wenching reprobate. Maybe it was the drinking and wenching that appealed to Connolly, but the part – as Callow had played it, at least – also involved a degree of nudity. The man who could happily discuss his bodily functions until the cows came home now had to display his body to a paying audience.

Cruel critics might have said that the audience could demand a refund after seeing Connolly in the raw, but on opening night the biggest shock wasn't the full-frontal flash, but the sight of his ears. Connolly had had a haircut. Whether the chop was done to distract the audience was not clear, but Connolly was clearly eager to reveal a new look, one way or another.

What with films, television and the stage, Connolly seemed to be accepting that he was a celebrity. He didn't necessarily like it, but he could certainly understand the public's interest in him. As he said in an interview, 'People have even stolen washing from the line. But If I'd known where Elvis hung up his shirts I would have nicked one.'

Perhaps he was beginning to mellow. He even did a school programme, *Androcles and the Lion.* Could Billy the Clydeside welder ever have predicted that in January 1983 Billy the entertainer would be appearing in the *TV Times Celebrity Knitting* book, modelling a jumper and gloves? There was a smile on Connolly's face, but just in case his friends thought he was going soft, he was posing so that you could see that the knuckles of his gloves had the words 'Love' and 'Hate' stitched onto them.

Maybe there was a reason for this new strictly cerebral hard man. Like Connolly, Pamela Stephenson also had a reputation for living life to the full, but since they had got together they seemed to have had a calming influence on each other. The relationship certainly seemed a success (and today they are still together and have three daughters), although cynics might not have given it much of a chance.

Although Stephenson had been born in New Zealand, she had grown up in Australia. You wouldn't have thought Connolly had much time for Australians, given that he once remarked that they were well-balanced people because they had a chip on each shoulder. Yet she seemed to have tamed this wild man of the north. He now even claimed he liked doing the dishes.

It also transpired that in 1981 Connolly had cut back on the booze and got into Buddhism. With the help of friends he had learnt to meditate. He was less agressive, more relaxed. As long as you weren't a member of the press, he was unlikely to lose his temper with you in public. He hadn't lost his sense of humour, though. As he once pointed out: 'I knew it was going to be a bad day. My karma ran over my dogma.'

Pamela Stephenson also helped Connolly to sort out his dressing habits once and for all. And not before time, either.

BELOW
**The Connolly of the '80s:
The tea-drinking years.**

(He was particularly concerned about itchy bottoms, and wondered why they always occurred in public and at the least convenient times. As Connolly observed with great relish, you never get an itchy bum in the middle of a desert. The comic suggested a few options, which included trying funny walks and clenching your buttocks, before suggesting the ultimate solution: to own up very loudly to having an itchy bum, so that everyone looks away in embarrassment and you can deal with it in private.)

RIGHT
Connolly joked that without his beard he couldn't get a table at Langans. Of course, knowing Michael Caine, one of the partners, probably helped.

In July 1983 he was voted one of Britain's Worst Dressed Men, finding himself in the company of Patrick Moore, Jim Davidson and Willie Rushton. Then again, given that the winners of the Best Dressed Man Award were Steve Davis, Terry Wogan and Ernie Wise, maybe he wasn't in such bad company after all.

By the autumn of 1983 Connolly was back on the road again. He didn't have a support act, choosing instead to break up the sheer force of his gags with a spot of banjo-picking. Since his folk days, music had become less and less a part of his act but, like an old comfort blanket, he picked it up whenever the mood took him, incorporating the moment into another comic routine: 'This is where three hundred people say, as if with one voice, 'Oh no, the bastard's going to sing.' And indeed he did, but it was a long way from playing 'The Wild Rover' in half-empty pubs to 'How can I tell you that I love you when you are sitting on my face?' in front of 2,000 fans, who ranged from silver-haired grannies to green-haired punks.

It was during the tour that Connolly celebrated his forty-first birthday. The days of carousing far into the alcoholic night were fast becoming little more than a memory and an occasional lapse. He claimed to have given up drinking when he realised that English had become his second language: 'after slurring'. As if to mark the change, his old sparring partner Michael Parkinson sent him a magnum of sparkling water, marked: 'For the man who has drunk everything.'

In 1984 Connolly had another crack at a movie (and, as with *Absolution,* unwittingly seemed to be single-handedly killing off the last dregs of the British film industry). This time round his co-star was Michael Caine, a man who, it has been jokingly said, has been known to choose his roles on the basis of the location for the shoot. This broad comedy, written by the creators of the classic

~

sitcom *The Likely Lads,* Clement and La Frenais, was set in the West Indies. Connolly played a Che Guevara-like rebel, Delgado Fitzhugh, who had chosen to sing to his people until his island was freed from the ruling dictators. Eventually he becomes President and gets to sing to the United Nations, so it seemed like an attractive, heroic role for the Scot. Ian La Frenais and Dick Clement had Billy in mind when they were writing the part, and Connolly certainly grabbed the role by the scruff, donning his fatigues and adding a touch of the Marx Brothers to this revolutionary Marxist.

ABOVE
**Comedy's royal couple:
Connolly and Stephenson
looking regal.**

❛ Photographers are that magic breed of men who sit on top of your roof with a telephoto lens and then accuse you of being a publicity-seeker. The most constructive thing they can do is file down the top of their camera to make it easier to shove up their arse. ❜

~

**Do you know a good baby-sitter?
Connolly chats with friends and
neighbours, the Duke and
Duchess of York, while Oliver
Reed looks on.**

Maybe it was the Caribbean climate, maybe it was the euphoria brought about by acting with one of British cinema's living legends, maybe it was the fact that in the film he got to sing in a band featuring Eric Clapton and Ringo Starr, but when he was interviewed on location by *You Magazine*, Connolly seemed particularly happy with his life and had few regrets about stardom: 'I've done it and I love it. It has its drawbacks, but when it comes to being noticed by people in the street, it is quite lovely. I would hate to have been born, lived and died and nobody noticed. It's proof that you exist, that all that practising with the banjo in your bedroom paid off.'

Michael Caine also spoke perceptively, but very highly, of his co-star: 'With Billy you know it's going to be funny, even before he starts. Billy doesn't have the eyes of a comedian – he has very dramatic eyes, they're almost savage. It's not only his humour that people identify with – it's his anger too. I wouldn't want to get on the wrong side of him.'

Sadly the film was a turkey, but if it ever crops up buried in the late-night schedules, it is worth seeing just to experience something extremely rare – an appearance from Billy Connolly that will not make you laugh.

Connolly's career had been one of steady progress interrupted by frequent bouts of rapid progress. If the constant in his life was his touring, he had also always been looking for other

~

ABOVE
Shooting stars: Connolly and Princess Anne got on well, but Connolly kept thinking about her face being on postage stamps.

OPPOSITE
Journalists beware! Shooting was always a hobby back in Glasgow – now he shot with the country's best marksmen.

avenues: writing and acting on film, stage and television. In 1984 he even had a chance to air some of his act on television in an LWT special, *A Weekend in Wallop*, but it still only hinted at the comic vulgarity of his live show. Filmed in a small village called Wallop, Connolly joined fellow comedians, including young turks Rowan Atkinson and Rik Mayall, under canvas. Connolly seemed keen to out-shock these young upstarts. In front of a rather sedate audience he offered his X-rated guide to masturba-tion. Connolly claimed to have come up with the perfect excuse to use, if caught 'counting your winnings'. The comic said you should pretend that a huge penis-eating spider had run up your trouser leg and you had removed your trousers in an effort to get the spider out, before it did too much irreparable damage. Inevitably the show attracted a fair number of complaints even though – equally inevitably – some of Connolly's choicer moments had been cut from the programme before it was deemed fit for home-viewing consumption.

Connolly could do shows in front of an English audience in his sleep and still bring the house down. He really needed to move on. In everything he had tried Connolly had tasted a certain amount of success, except when it came to America. It was a strange kind of love-hate relationship. Connolly, with his bright, loud shirts and extrovert stage manner, was attracted to the brashness of

ABOVE
**Billy and Pamela at the
wedding of the Duke and
Duchess of York in 1986.**

this young country, which seemed so full of vitality after the dour, grey porridge-like atmosphere of Glasgow. He didn't like to fail and was not happy that his biggest shows to date in the USA had been as the support act to Elton John; what chance did the lone Scottish comedian have when faced with an audience baying for the balding balladeer in an array of spectacular outfits? A few years after his tour with Elton, Connolly reflected on the experience in *Time Out* and put his failure onstage in America down to the nation's narcotic habits: 'The problem with American audiences is that they are all on drugs and everyone's going at a different pace. Some of them are so high on Quaaludes they can't see, never mind hear you.'

Undaunted though, he was determined to crack America, whatever it took: 'Over there they don't even know I've been born. I'd even shave my beard off, if I had to. Actually I have this overwhelming desire to see what's living there underneath it. I'd be prepared to do away with it for the right role.'

In a particularly candid interview, Connolly also made quite clear his feelings about the paparazzi who had haunted him since his separation from his wife: 'Photographers are that magic breed of men who sit on top of your roof with a telephoto lens and then accuse you of being a publicity-seeker. The most constructive thing they can do is file down the top of their camera to make it easier to shove up their arse.'

~

By the mid-'80s Connolly seemed financially secure, and domestically secure with Pamela Stephenson. All those years on the road had left him with a healthy bank balance, and in August 1986 the couple moved from west London to their estate in Bray in Berkshire, part-stockbroker belt, part-showbiz suburb (neighbours included Rolf Harris, Michael Parkinson and Terry Wogan). Despite the house being set in its own land, Connolly needed more space – according to the tabloids, he also rented an allotment on which to grow his cabbages.

After a couple of years, however, Connolly wanted to move on and purchased something even grander in Windsor. He now lived near to, and socialised with, the Duke and Duchess of York. It seemed like an unlikely friendship to those who had Connolly down for life as the socialist welder from Glasgow. But Connolly the non-conformist probably revelled in the irony (and maybe he was secretly quite flattered by the royal interest in him). He was certainly not about to make any attempt to fit in, dubbing his new stately pile Grunt Futtock Hall, after a character that Kenneth Williams used to play in the radio show *Round the Horne*. William the Conqueror was master of all he surveyed. But he was now looking across the Atlantic and had seen something there that he wanted to take on, too.

BELOW
**William the Conqueror
meets Princess Di in 1988.**

CHAPTER FIVE

AMERICA: LEAD-FREE AND FART-FREE

*B*y 1987 Connolly was determined to crack America. In an echo of his famous breakthrough on Michael Parkinson's chat-show, he seemed to be attempting to make his mark on the USA as a guest on the American equivalent, *The Late Show with Joan Rivers*, by talking to her about his sexual education: 'When I was a child I was lousy at school and I used to look out the window watching the pigeons making love on the roof opposite. They make love very quickly, pigeons. I based my whole sex life on that. I'm very good and very fast.'

LEFT
**Connolly plans his
assault on America.**

OPPOSITE
**More tea, vicar? Connolly
about to enter sitcom-land.**

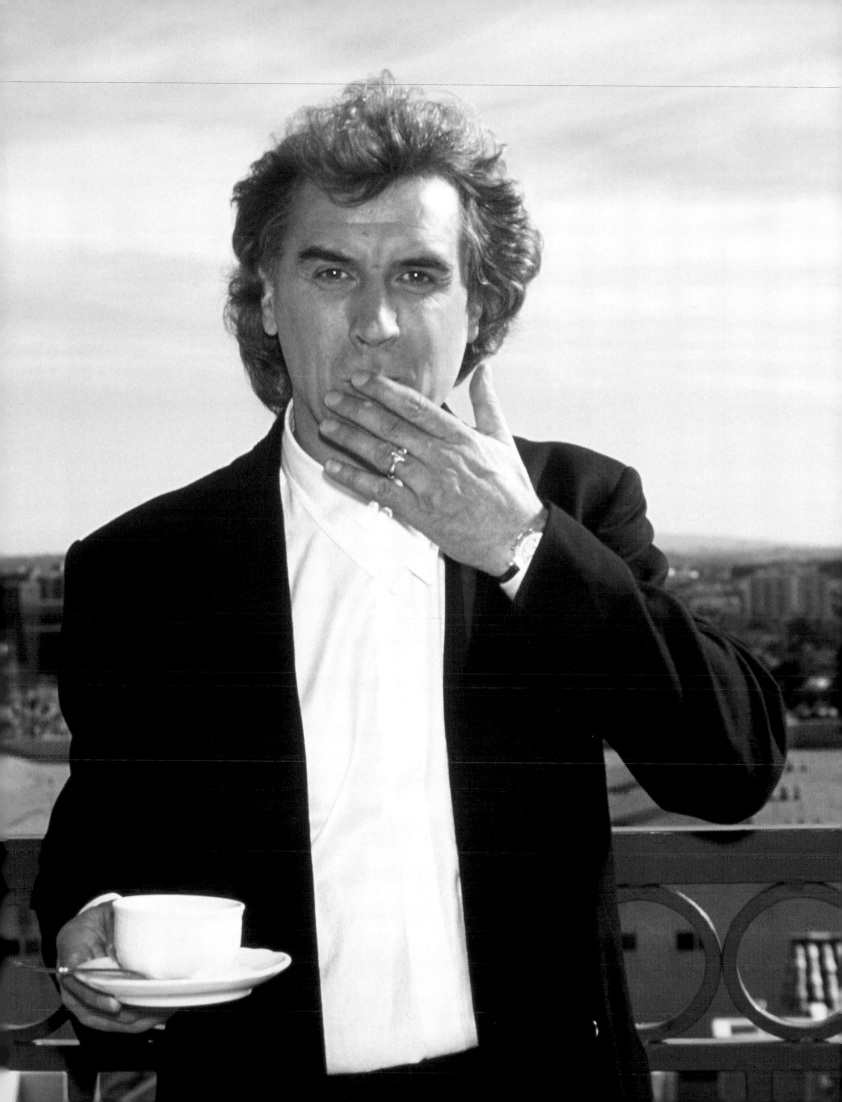

AIDS was the big story of the time and, with safe sex being advocated, Connolly took on the topic of condoms, asking Joan Rivers when the best time to put one on was, if you were on a date. Connolly didn't get an answer, but concluded that it wasn't as soon as you arrive at the house.

Connolly was lucky in that most of his act travelled well. The only material he was using in England that he couldn't use in America related to specifically English things. Putting his stall out back home, alongside the likes of Ben Elton and Alexei Sayle, Connolly would attack the old school of showbiz trouper, asking, for instance, how Bob Monkhouse and Des O'Connor got so shiny (did they, perhaps, go to shiny school?). In America his material had to be more up-front, and in some ways more politicised. The world, as well as Connolly, was now a very different prospect compared to twenty years earlier. If there had ever been a hint of sexism in his '70s shows, the pendulum had now swung the other way and Connolly had a post-feminist stance – women now wanted multiple orgasms, men had to give them to them, and women would tell men when to stop.

It is interesting to compare Connolly's enthusiasm for America in the late '80s with remarks he made about America in 1976 in *Billy Connolly – The Authorised Version*. At that time he had only performed on his own, mixing music and comedy, and had not yet been a support artist for Elton John, and his impressions were strictly negative: 'I've always found travelling around the States very strange. You keep arriving in places at the same time as you left the last place, and you've always got the wrong clothes on. And then you are expected to get up and play. Like at this Irish club, where I was expected to play for a crowd of decrepit Irish cowboys.

ABOVE
An artist of a higher calibre: Connolly brilliantly parodies the Wonderbra campaign.

OPPOSITE
The heady quiff of celebrity.

'When I got to the club I was completely wiped out, and I was meant to go on at half-past six. But there's not a soul in the club. All you can see are those little candles in glasses that they have in American night clubs. Just those and the barmen. At half-past six the manager comes over to me. "You're on." "But there's nobody here." "This is America. You're on." Quite amazing. So I sang. And not even the barmen bothered to listen.'

Not surprisingly, in 1976 Connolly wasn't that keen to return. But the remarkable irony is that he went on to single out a particular part of America as a no-go area. 'There are some bits of America I can't take at all. Like Los Angeles. Everyone is going around saying how wonderful

❛ When I got to the club I was completely wiped out and I was meant to go on at half-past six. But there's not a soul in the club. All you can see are those little candles in glasses that they have in American night clubs. Just those and the barmen. At half-past six the manager comes over to me. "You're on." "But there's nobody here." "This is America. You're on." Quite amazing. So I sang. And not even the barmen bothered to listen.❜

everything is and how wonderful everybody is..."I really love ya." Phone-ey. I much prefer the madness of New York.' Little did Connolly realise at the time that he was little more than a decade away from setting up home in Los Angeles.

Connolly didn't become an instant star in America, but he had tested the waters and had a positive response. His strategy now was to do what rock bands such as the Police had done. He went out on the road, playing any and every town in America. Sometimes it seemed as if he was always on the road, in an aeroplane or stuck in a hotel, but he felt that this was the only way he could make an impression. It felt as if he was starting all over again, accepting bookings for expenses only.

He also came back to England to do a job without giving any consideration to the fee. In 1989 Connolly showed a more serious side in a film made for Comic Relief. In it he travelled to Mozambique and movingly showed how the African state was coping with a war that had been raging since independence from Portugal in 1975. In 1995 he went back to the land that one of his daughters called 'Nose and Beak' and caught up with some of the survivors of the fighting. Few who saw the film can forget that Connolly, maybe for the first time in his career, was actually lost for words, when on-camera a man returned to his village to be reunited with the few surviving members of his family.

Connolly took part in Comic Relief because it was something he believed in. There was not a grain of cynicism in his appearance, but it did keep his television profile up. Connolly's battle with British TV seemed to have

BELOW
Laugh? I thought my bow tie would explode.

ABOVE
Success on a different plane: airport duty with Pamela and Daisy, Amy and Scarlett.

reached a stalemate. He wouldn't attempt to do the juicy bits of his act, and it would constantly invite him onto its chat-shows and give him a chance to rattle off some milder anecdotes in between giggling fits.

Connolly's most memorable performances have been on talk-shows, even though in the *Guardian* in 1989 he claimed not to be a talk-show person: 'I only go on to appear windswept and interesting. People say to me you could have a series. I would no more have a TV series than a nail in my forehead. I've never wanted it and I don't want it now.' Over the next seven years and over two continents, these were words that someone ought to have served to him on a plate, with some garnish and a knife and fork.

In 1989, when Connolly was asked to appear in another movie, *The Big Man*, he had to make a dramatic change to his appearance. The beard finally had to go for the role of a Mr Fixit of the bare-knuckle-fight world, and with it the appearance of a caveman. Until now Connolly had spent most of his adult life looking like some neanderthal who had swallowed a bear and still had the tongue flopping out of his mouth and over his chin. Now clean-shaven for the first time in twenty-six years, he revealed a dimple worthy of Kirk Douglas. Not surprisingly, this was a shock to Connolly, who looked in the mirror and thought he was wearing somebody else's face. It did have its pluses, though. For a while the paparazzi didn't recognise him and he could walk through London relatively unhassled, which was a good thing. A bad thing, according to Connolly, was that he was now

~

OPPOSITE
Caught on camera and looking windswept and interesting at Sting's wedding.

so anonymous that he had difficulty getting a table at celebrity restaurant Langans. The clean shave was not a decision taken lightly. It can't have been easy to remove the beard, which had become a kind of lucky charm over the years. It had saved his skin, quite literally, at least once. Back in Glasgow one time when the beard was longer, a man had attempted to punch Connolly on the chin. He aimed for the bottom of the beard, thinking the chin would be underneath, but swang and found himself jabbing at thin air. Now Connolly would have to defend himself without this facial armour. It also wasn't easy in a very literal sense – Connolly did not actually know how to shave that part of his face and had a few bloody accidents before he got it as smooth as a baby's bum.

If the de-bearding wasn't symbolic enough, in December 1989 Connolly married Pamela Stephenson in a place where very few people indeed would recognise him, beard or no beard. With their three young daughters, Daisy, Amy and Scarlett, and Barry Humphries among the guests, Billy and Pamela married on the island of Fiji. Anyone who was thinking that Connolly had lost his sense of humour should have been there. Instead of the usual wedding hymns, the ceremony was topped off by a piped rendition of the theme music from the *Archers*.

It is easy, in retrospect, to see why 1989 became such a pivotal year for Connolly in terms of his decision to concentrate on America. Ten years on from the arrival of Margaret Thatcher as Prime Minister, he must have felt rather dispirited by the state of England. While he was not the most party political of comics, he had lent his support to the Labour Party and in 1989 they still seemed to be a long way from an election victory.

But it wasn't just the political situation that contributed to his decision to concentrate his efforts elsewhere. While Connolly had constantly failed to make much headway in terms of television, he had accepted the situation as confirmation that he was too 'dangerous'. Suddenly, now, all the other younger dangerous comedians were becoming superstars. Ben Elton, Harry Enfield, Rowan Atkinson, 'The Young Ones' and the entire *Comic Strip* alumni had become the new comedy establishment. And of course they all owed a debt to Connolly, who had paved the way for them, only to be left behind. They were getting all the credibility for taking risks, yet often all they were doing was getting laughs by being infantile and saying 'pooh' and 'bum', words that Connolly had specialised in. There may have been some acute, sophisticated observational humour in the work of Ben Elton and Harry Enfield, but Connolly's influence was undeniable, though invariably it went unacknowledged.

While Lenny Henry, who also predated the *Comic Strip*, had adapted his act and married Dawn French and suddenly found himself part of the new set, Connolly didn't need to adapt his act because he had never been that different. Connolly has never admitted that a sense of isolation or frustration was a reason for his departure from Britain, but it must have played its part. In the

absence of an award-winning show, it is a lot easier to look like an elder statesman of alternative comedy when you are trotting out *bon mots* on the *Clive James Show* live via satellite from sunny Los Angeles 5,000 miles away.

Whatever the reasons, all that slogging to and from Gutbucket, Arizona and Footrot, Alabama was beginning to pay off as the '80s turned into the '90s. If Billy Connolly had been looking for a television breakthrough, it looked as if he had found it when, following an impressive appearance on a Whoopi Goldberg special, he was signed up to play the teacher in the sitcom *Head of the Class*. Many British comics, ranging from Peter Cook to Alexei Sayle, have been involved in American sit-coms, but neither Cook nor Sayle, for instance, had established themselves in America through their acting. Connolly had an advantage, in that he was joining a proven success. The previous American star, Howard Hesseman, was leaving, but because the series was a hit the producers wanted to keep it going.

Whether it was to make the part easier for Connolly to get into, the writers didn't make the character that different from Billy's real self, with a touch of the American dream thrown in for good measure: teacher Billy McGregor was a former shipyard worker who had – please suspend

OPPOSITE
More Connolly at Sting's.

RIGHT
Billy and Pamela display the latest addition to the clan.

your sanity for a moment, and remember this is Hollywood – pulled himself up by his bootstraps, studied at Oxford and gone to work as an academic in America. Then again, wasn't the real Billy Connolly a symbol of the American dream? The former welder turned world superstar, whose kids played with the offspring of the Duke and Duchess of York? It's amazing the scriptwriters didn't just turn Connolly's real life into a comedy and call it something like *Meet the Duke*, or *My Prince Next Door*.

BELOW
**Happy families with Pamela
and Daisy, Amy and Scarlett.**

❛ Until now Connolly had spent most of his adult life looking like some Neanderthal who had swallowed a bear and still had the tongue flopping out of his mouth and over his chin. Now clean shaven for the first time in twenty-six years, he revealed a dimple worthy of Kirk Douglas. Not surprisingly, this was a shock to Connolly, who looked in the mirror and thought he was wearing somebody else's face. ❜

Connolly seemed to like America. He liked the Californian climate, he liked his own parking space with his name on it in the Warner Brothers parking lot. He liked having his own caravan to relax in when he wasn't filming. If there were fears that California was going to smooth over Connolly's cruder edges, they seemed unfounded. On the door of his trailer was a sticker that said 'lead-free and fart-free'. Only one person could have put it there.

Connolly filmed twenty-two episodes of *Head of the Class* and Warner Brothers clearly thought they had a hit and a star on their hands, signing up Connolly as part of a lucrative deal. A few months later, however, *Head of the Class* was cancelled, though no blame was placed on Connolly. Warners showed their confidence in him by starting to develop a new sitcom. The film *Green Card* had recently been a success and this was a television variant, with Billy playing a Scot who has to marry an American to stay in the country.

By 1992, when *Billy* was transmitted, Connolly and his family had moved into a luxurious home in the Hollywood Hills. One of his neighbours was David Hockney, while Errol Flynn had also lived nearby. Connolly socialised with the most successful ex-pats – Connery, Caine, Elton John. Gene Kelly's granddaughter used to play with his daughters. If life seemed good, the series didn't. It was panned by the critics, though fortunately more for its hackneyed format and lack of chemistry than for Connolly's performance. Critics still predicted big things for Billy the comic, but predicted an early demise for *Billy* the show. It actually ran for thirteen episodes, before it was axed in June 1992. It was probably the most humane decision.

The temporary end of the American television sojourn meant that Connolly was a gob for hire again. Later in 1992 he found himself working in Hollywood alongside two of the town's biggest stars, Demi Moore and Robert Redford. Well, maybe working alongside them was a bit grand, but they were in the same scene in *Indecent Proposal*. For some reason best known to British director Adrian Lyne, Connolly played a celebrity auctioneer at a charity auction in, of all places, a zoo. It was a quick role and while British viewers might have had a chuckle at the sight of Connolly in such illustrious company, in America it must have been seen somewhat differently. Connolly wasn't famous enough there for the role to be a celebrity cameo, but he was clearly too distinctive a person for it to have been a bit-part. In many ways it was the perfect reflection of his own position over there, where he was a medium-sized fish in a huge pool. Then again, one of the attractions of America is obviously the fact that even medium-sized fish can afford mansions in the Hollywood Hills. It was an odd position to be in, for a man who had been a rip-roaring success for twenty years and was now approaching his fiftieth birthday. So how does someone like that celebrate their fiftieth birthday? Easy, really. Connolly went out and had his nipples pierced.

CHAPTER SIX

GOING BACK TO PISS ON OLD TREES

I f Connolly's position in America hung in the balance following his mixed fortunes, he was still clearly a star in Britain, albeit an absentee one. In between American TV work he had toured Britain and was still able to pack out theatres everywhere, but he was still looking for other challenges. In 1993 he teamed up for the third time with playwright Peter McDougall. This time round the BBC drama was Down Among the Big Boys, *a hard-hitting yet comic drama set in Glasgow's gangland. Connolly had been cast as Jo Jo Donnelly, the father of a girl who was about to marry a policeman. As if this wasn't bad enough, Donnelly was also planning a big bank job, which his prospective son-in-law was supposed to be investigating. The highlight of this richly observed comedy was the scene in which Connolly and his cohorts exploded their way into the vaults, timing the bangs to coincide with the drums of a street march going on outside. Scorcese's* Good-Fellas *hadn't shown big-time crime any better. And another comparison with* Good-Fellas: *for a change Connolly could be seen wearing some unusually smart, if sober, suits. He was into his fifties now, and pierced nipples or no pierced nipples, he was beginning to look his age.*

OPPOSITE
The William Wallace of the wellie and wee-wee brigade: Connolly in warrior mode.

It wasn't quite clear what he was doing to his hair, but every time he appeared on television it seemed a slightly different colour. At one point he looked like an ageing badger, with a grey streak down the middle; another time he looked like sports presenter Dickie Davies, whose coiffure Connolly had actually sent up in the past, saying that he looked as if he had been painting the ceiling white and some of the emulsion had dripped onto him. The Hair Gods were clearly now having their revenge on Connolly, who spoke movingly of the changes going on below his waistband.

Connolly had always been one taboo ahead of the pack, and now that other comedians were happily talking about willies, Connolly turned to pubic hair. He revealed on television that his was now turning grey. In a certain light his penis now resembled Stewart Granger. Connolly liked to call it distinguished. It also proved that age may have taken its toll in some respects, but it hadn't withered his ability to come up with new ways of shocking his fans.

In middle age Connolly had adapted his approach, so that he wasn't so much an angry young man as a middle-aged curmudgeon. Still on the subject of hair, he was a veritable swearing version of Victor Meldrew when it came to choosing what kind of shampoo to buy, when faced with a row full of choice in the supermarket. Connolly was particularly puzzled by Jojoba. 'In Scotland that's the month before November.'

Just as confusing was the range of flavours on offer. To Connolly, egg and mushroom, or avocado and walnut, were more suited to the frying pan than to the bathroom. And as for shampoos for greasy hair, normal hair or dry hair, he just wanted shampoo for dirty hair. Egg and mushroom, avocado and walnut. What happened to soap?

Like an ageing footballer who makes up with instinctive skills what he lacks in pace, Connolly adapted his material brilliantly. He also revealed insights into his early days that might have seemed inappropriate a decade or two earlier. Connolly had always had a remarkable memory, and when he talked about the doctor examining his own prostate gland, it reminded him of a man called Cassidy who used to work at Stephen's Yard thirty years earlier, who would always complain about his prostate. At the time Connolly didn't understand him – in fact, as the doctor approached him, he was still hoping the prostate was somewhere like the elbow – but now, at about the same age, he knew exactly where the prostate was and what Cassidy had been talking about.

Surprisingly, Connolly never got much material out of the

ABOVE
**Older, but not much wiser on
the trouser front.**

~

86

RIGHT
**Laughing all the
way to the bank.**

(I'm the least
subversive man on
earth. I'd love to be, but
they confuse cause and
effect. In the same way,
I don't think the films
of that big, silly Austrian
Schwarzenegger make
people kill one another.)

childhood of his first two children, but the births of his family with Pamela Stephenson seemed to open the funny-bone floodgates. Or maybe it wasn't so much the children as the technology that is part and parcel of having children in the '90s. Connolly's essential advice is never to get a baby alarm, because once you do your baby will learn how to pretend to die. It may not sound all that funny, but Connolly does a marvellous impression of sitting downstairs, reading casually while the baby gurgles away upstairs, and then going into a blind panic the moment the gurgling stops. It's a visual, sound-effect-based routine that shows Connolly has lost none of his early knack for non-verbal communication – except that in the past his speciality was farting, belching and vomiting. It must be at least a decade since he did any gags about throwing up – searching for Hughie and Ralph (you have to shout and maybe cough the names to get the joke). In fact Hughie and Ralph's demise probably coincided with the comic giving up alcohol.

~

In middle age Connolly seemed to be working harder than ever. In an interview during his early success he had said that he had been tempted to stop, and thought that he might 'buy a wee shop and sell Smarties to children, or make muffins at Loch Lomond. But you must constantly stretch your imagination. If you stop, you die.' The second part of this philosophy seemed truer than ever, even though he and his family were now financially secure for life. Connolly was behaving like a shark that had been wounded. As long as he kept swimming he would survive, but the moment he paused, he would go under. And intriguingly Connolly has clearly been working for job satisfaction rather than the money in recent years – you can tell that by the number of projects he has undertaken for the BBC – not an organisation that is well known for being a big spender.

The other notable thing about Connolly's '90s output is how so much of it has had a Scottish angle. It is as if, after years of difficulties in knowing how to deal with his homeland, he has just given a metaphorical shrug, said 'Oh fuck it', given Scotland a hug and come home.

After *Down Among the Big Boys* he returned to Scotland to make an arts documentary series, *The Bigger Picture*, which looked at the history of Scottish art. Here was one Monarch of the Glen showing that there was more to Scottish art than simply shortbread tins and the original 'Monarch of the Glen'. It was quite an education for Connolly too, who remarked with unusual seriousness that, 'I now know there's a great deal more to Scottish art than pictures of the growling mountains of Glencoe on shortbread tins.' He even started collecting

OPPOSITE
Entering middle age disgracefully.

RIGHT
The eternal child.

RIGHT
Casual yet smart. Billy and Pamela out on the town.

indigenous art, including some works by Glasgow-mate-made-good, writer of *Tutti Frutti* and fellow beardy, John Byrne.

In 1994 he continued to visit old haunts, setting up a tour that went all the way round the villages and community centres all over Scotland. He now seemed prepared to admit that there was an element of nostalgia in his game plan, remarking that it was 'important to keep doing it where I started'. But he was quick to back up this spot of romance with a punchline that reminded his fans that this was Billy Connolly talking: 'It's good to go back and piss on the old trees occasionally.'

The country tour was filmed for the BBC as part of *Billy Connolly's World Tour of Scotland*. This latest way of tackling the problem of Connolly's material found him mixing clips of his stand-up act (dressed in remarkably sober black) with a travelogue, as Connolly talked us around Scotland like the wittiest, most passionate tour guide you are ever likely to encounter. While the programme must have done wonders for the tourist industry, his comedy was still causing problems. Apart from the expected high-expletive count, Connolly had also attempted to do some topical material about the recent Fred West murder case, which received complaints.

Having road-tested his act, however, it was a well-oiled comedy machine that reached the Hammersmith Apollo, one packed with surreal insights, as Connolly asked who discovered that we could get milk from cows – and what were they doing at the time? Or do parrots ever get sick as a football manager? Anyone who might have dared suggest that Connolly was burnt-out or past it was quickly proved wrong. His run was extended and he appeared there for a record-breaking twenty-four nights.

OPPOSITE
Connolly joins Robin Williams and Dudley Moore at Langans.

So is Billy Connolly becoming respectable? Well, yes. And then again, no. While he has been known to entertain Prince Charles at

Windsor, he still has that irreverent streak, which he will never shake off. While he was invited to present the BAFTA Awards in 1995, this didn't stop him from sending up the ceremony. And he does have a fondness for appearing in the nude in public, which is hardly a sign of maturity. He did it during the filming of *Billy Connolly's World Tour of Scotland* and he indulged in it again – taking a great personal risk with his genitals – when he was the subject of *A Scot in the Arctic* in 1995.

Earlier that year the BBC had a great success with *Girl Friday*, in which Joanna Lumley was left on a desert island and the cameras followed her struggle with the elements. In the follow-up – which sounded suspiciously as if they came up with the title first and then approached Billy – Connolly had to spend six days alone on the freezing Ellesmere Island off Greenland. It seemed like a long way to go to avoid the press.

Connolly embraced the project, which climaxed with him stripping off, jumping out of his tent and running through the snow naked, baring his bottom for an audience in the name of art, just as he had done all those years ago in *The Beastly Beatitudes of Balthazar B.*

It was a breathtakingly beautiful sight – the Arctic, not his arse – but there were also polar bears to contend with. Connolly was further worried by the tall stories that the Eskimos were telling him. The production team had egged them on, but maybe they went a little too far, and things were not made any easier when a Texan hunter passed by, towing a dead ten-foot-bear.

At the end of the filming Connolly had few regrets about the project. He had grown as a person, become stronger within himself and had also been given a seal-skin suit by the local Eskimos, which he brought back to auction off for charity. Unfortunately the skin hadn't been cured and after two days it stank out the office and had to be binned.

Which brings us, and Billy Connolly, to 1996. Twenty-five years on from his first solo gig in Musselburgh, he shows few signs of slowing down. In May he was honoured by the BBC, who let him schedule an evening's programmes. Funnily enough, a lot of them were Billy Connolly programmes. It must have been somewhat like having your life flash by in front of you, but Connolly was far from finished. He was still restoring links with Scotland when he appeared as Deacon Brodie in the eponymous BBC drama, which was shown in a special gala screening at the Edinburgh Film Festival.

It was obviously a role that appealed to Connolly. Brodie was an eighteenth-century councillor who was hanged on a gibbet of his own design for robbing banks to fund his womanising. He was said to have inspired Robert Louis Stevenson's *Dr Jekyll and Mr Hyde*. Like Connolly, this cabinet maker, deacon and gambler had a complex psychological make-up. Talking to the *Guardian*, Connolly admitted that he could see the connection: 'The split personality thing appeals to me very much. He stole money when he didn't need it and squandered the dough anyway. He did it for the excitement. Brodie is a wee bit out of control. He's a bit of a nutter in fact. I like people like that. I like it in myself.'

❛ The split personality thing appeals to me very much. Brodie (the 18th century councillor who robbed banks to fund his womanising) stole money when he didn't need it and squandered the dough anyway. He did it for the excitement. Brodie is a wee bit out of control. He's a bit of a nutter in fact. I like people like that. I like it in myself ❜

CONNOLLY ON
DEAN BRODIE.

LEFT
**Hail the conquering hero.
Connolly returns to his
native Scotland.**

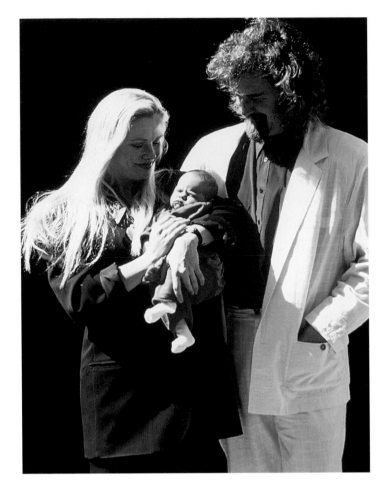

There were obvious comparisons to be made with Connolly's own life, so Connolly made them before the press did. Continuing to talk to the *Guardian,* it wasn't clear at first whether Connolly was talking about Brodie's life or his own contradictions: 'They say he dines with the Queen but is supposed to be a rebel. He's friendly with posh people, therefore he can't like his background any more. He doesn't live in Scotland, therefore he doesn't like Scotland. They have the weirdest view of me. I can't fight it any more.'

Connolly seemed resigned to being pigeonholed, but made one last plea to be understood as someone with more than one side to his character: 'I believe duality is a very strong trait in Celtic men, the poet and the warrior being in the same person. I knew men on the Clyde who were like that – very poetic, extremely well-read men who were also very hard men, who wouldn't think twice about smacking people in the mouth.'

In closing, Connolly became unusually philosophical about his craft: 'We comedians are the most lonely people in the world. It's like being on the moon out there. If you make a mistake you die. But it's brilliant. You are like an outlaw, you create your own reality, your own rules.'

Connolly continues to make his own rules. And he was finally discovering that television was coming round to his way of looking at things. Following the success of his *World Tour of Scotland,* the BBC made a *World Tour of Australia* – same principle, better weather. And Connolly was also talking about playing John Brown, Queen Victoria's faithful retainer, in a new drama, which will no doubt inspire more ill-informed, opinionated journalists to dust down those cuttings and ramble on about Connolly dining with the Yorks and chatting with Prince Charles.

Say what you like about Connolly, when he has been choosing non-stand-up work he has had a habit of choosing jobs that will notch up plenty of attention and controversy in the tabloids.

If everything goes to plan, Connolly will be positively ubiquitous as he kicks off his second quarter-century in comedy. There was talk of him replacing Bob Hoskins in the British Telecom ad campaign, following Connolly's great success spoofing the Wonderbra ads in his non-alcoholic Kaliber commercial. In the end, Connolly won't be telling us, 'It's good to talk'. Instead he has his eyes set on bigger things. He may well do more acting, he may well go back to Hollywood. He has mentioned that he might move out to Australia where he has always had a huge following. But wherever Connolly goes in the English-speaking world, he will always be a superstar. At a time when their is endless muttering about a single currency, Connolly already has one in spades – it is called 'the gift of the gab'.

RIGHT

For once Connolly has his lips sealed. With big things in the pipeline, they won't be for much longer.

⟨ We comedians are the most lonely people in the world. It's like being on the moon out there. If you make a mistake you die. But it's brilliant. You are like an outlaw, you create your own reality, your own rules. ⟩

ACKNOWLEDGEMENTS

Many thinks to everyone too humorous to mention who assisted me in the compilation of this book. In particular many thanks to my indulgent employers Time Out and to Cath, Lily and Florence, who stayed out of my way when necessary and laughed at Billy's jokes in all the right places when they were around.

PHOTOGRAPHIC CREDITS

ALL ACTION PICTURES
Page: 34 (D. Raban), 78.
REX FEATURES LTD.
Page: 6, 18, 19, 37, 54, 57, 61 (Richard Young),
65 (Richard Young), 70, 72 (Dave Lewis),
73, 74 (John Gooch), 75, 76 (Clive Dixon),
77, 80 (Dave Hartley), 81, 82, 85, 94, 95.
SYNDICATION INTERNATIONAL LTD.
Page: 7, 12, 13, 14, 25, 29, 40, 58, 60, 62/3, 64 (Darryl Estrine),
67, 68, 69, 71, 87, 90, 91, 93.
LONDON FEATURES INTERNATIONAL LTD.
Page: 21, 22, 23, 30, 31, 33 (Steve Rapport),
39 (Nick Elgar), 42 (Nick Elgar), 43 (Nick Elgar),
47, 49 (Steve Rapport), 66 (Gregg De Guire).
HULTON DEUTSCH COLLECTION LTD.
Page: 8, 9, 11 (Mike Moore), 15, 16, 17 (Mike Moore),
20, 24, 26, 27, 59 (Doug McKenzie).
RETNA PICTURES LTD.
Page: 28 (Michael Putland), 10 (Michael Putland),
38, 41 (Kevin Cummins), 46 (John Welsby),
48, 50 (Steve Rapport), 51 (Tobi Corney), 52 (Steve Rapport),
58, 86 (Darryl Estrine), 88.

~